SPORT
IN "QUOTES"

 I'm lucky because I have an athlete between my legs.

Willie Carson, Scottish jockey and television presenter, five times British Champion Jockey with 3,828 wins to his credit.

Alhaarth, ridden by Willie Carson, finishes ahead of the field in The Solario Stakes at Sandown Park, Esher, Surrey.
18th August, 1995

SPORT
IN "QUOTES"

AMMONITE
PRESS

PRESS
ASSOCIATION
Images

First Published 2011 by
Ammonite Press
an imprint of AE Publications Ltd,
166 High Street, Lewes, East Sussex BN7 1XU, United Kingdom

Reprinted 2012

ISBN 978-1-90667-259-1

British Cataloguing in Publication Data. A catalogue
record of this book is available from the British Library.

Editor: Ian Penberthy
Managing Editor: Richard Wiles
Picture research: Press Association Images
Design: Fineline Studios

Colour reproduction by GMC Reprographics
Printed and bound in China by 1010 Printing International Ltd

England's fast bowler Fred Trueman celebrates his team's victory with a pint and a cigarette: he took 11 wickets for 88 runs during the Ashes Third Test against Australia.
8th July, 1961

66 I'm an actress, I'm a model and I'm an athlete. I put athlete third on my list. **99**

Serena Williams, US tennis player, former World Number One, winner of 13 Grand Slam women's singles titles, 12 Grand Slam women's doubles titles and two Grand Slam mixed doubles titles, one of the greatest female players of all time.

USA's Serena Williams in action against Czech Republic's Petra Kvitova during the Lawn Tennis Championships at the All England Club, Wimbledon.
1st July, 2010

INTRODUCTION

Sportsmen and women have always been our everyday heroes, individuals who push themselves to the physical limit and beyond, striving for perfection and aiming to reach the top of their chosen sport, whether alone or as members of a team. We follow them through thick and thin, cheering them on and sharing in the joy of their triumphs, commiserating with them in the face of setbacks: like medieval knights, they are our champions, going forward into battle and carrying with them all our hopes for victory.

Because sportsmen and women are so inspirational and important to so many, it is inevitable that what they say often is almost as important as what they do, the more so in this modern age of celebrity. The vast world of sport is full of fascinating, intelligent, erudite and witty individuals, whose utterances can be inspirational, funny, moving or just plain quirky – who could forget, or fathom, Manchester United footballer Eric Cantona's reference to seagulls following trawlers? And presented in this book is but a small sample of quotes from a diverse group of characters from across the wide spectrum of sport, dating back to the turn of the 20th century, whether they be athletes, officials or commentators. Here, revealed in their own words, is their passion, their determination, their frustration, their joy in success and their sadness in failure – words, often poetic, sometimes unintentional, occasionally muddled, that inspire, encourage, inform, entertain, confuse and amuse.

Here we have BBC commentator Brian Johnston's comical descriptions of activity on the cricket pitch, the poetic predictions and comments of boxer Muhammad Ali, the verbal gaffes of sports commentators like David Coleman, the inspirational thoughts of gymnast Nadia Comeneci and runner Emil Zátopek, the good-natured ribbing of football manager Brian Clough, and much, much more.

Illustrating these bon mots and faux pas is a fascinating selection of photographs from the vast archives of the Press Association, whose skilled photographers have been present at every major sports fixture since the end of the 19th century, recording the action and the individuals who have given their all in their endeavour to achieve success in the sporting arena.

66 Who ate all the pies? 99

Sheffield United fans, to the tune of *Knees Up Mother Brown*, on William 'Fatty' Foulke, English goalkeeper of the late 19th and early 20th centuries, who was renowned for his great height (6ft 4in) and weight (said by some to be as much as 24 stone).

Bill 'Fatty' Foulke, Chelsea goalkeeper.
At school, Foulke had been a successful
athlete, nicknamed the 'Whippet'.
1894

" Charles Fry could be autocratic, angry and self-willed: he was also magnanimous, extravagant, generous, elegant, brilliant – and fun ... he was probably the most variously gifted Englishman of any age. "

John Arlott, cricket commentator, on Charles Burgess Fry, English sportsman, politician, diplomat and writer. Fry represented England at both cricket and football, and also was an accomplished long jumper.

C.B. Fry on crutches after injuring one of his ankles badly while playing for Sussex against Middlesex. *1908*

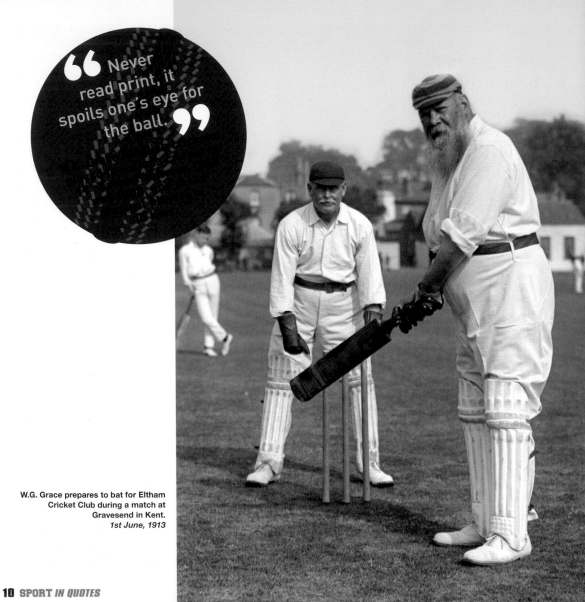

Never read print, it spoils one's eye for the ball.

W.G. Grace prepares to bat for Eltham
Cricket Club during a match at
Gravesend in Kent.
1st June, 1913

❝ If you'd been on your honeymoon, you couldn't have had a happier time. **❞**

Steve Donoghue, English jockey, ten times Champion Jockey, six times Derby winner, on winning Ascot's Queen Alexandra Stakes on Brown Jack, a feat he achieved for six consecutive years (1929–34).

Champion jockey Steve Donoghue (R) chats with World Flyweight boxing champion Jimmy Wilde during a race meeting at Windsor.
8th April, 1919

66 A snick by Jack Hobbs
is a sort of disturbance of a
cosmic orderliness. **99**

**Sir Neville Cardus, English writer
on cricket, on Jack Hobbs, English
cricketer, known as 'The Master',
who made 61 appearances for
England between 1908 and 1930,
the greatest ever opening batsman
in the history of the game.**

At the Oval cricket ground in South
London, Surrey batsman Jack Hobbs
demonstrates the skill that gained
him the nickname 'The Master'.
1925

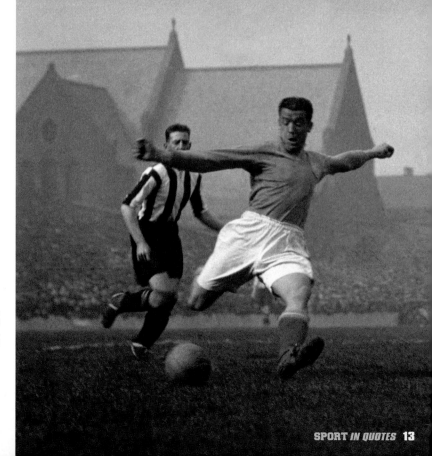

66 I'm going for a pee.
You coming? **99**

**Dixie Dean, English footballer, one of the
most prolific goal scorers in English football
history, scorer of 60 league goals during the
1927/28 season, to an over-enthusiastic marker.**

Bill 'Dixie' Dean of Everton shoots for
goal at his team's home ground of
Goodison Park.
20th October, 1930

66 I didn't aspire to be a good sport; 'champion' was good enough for me. **99**

Fred Perry, English tennis player, former World Number One, eight times Grand Slam winner, first player ever to win all four Grand Slam events.

Fred Perry lunges to play a backhand against Adrian Quist during the Wimbledon men's singles championships; Perry would win the final that year.
30th June, 1934

66 When I came back, after all those stories about Hitler and his snub, I came back to my native country, and I could not ride in the front of the bus. I had to go to the back door. I couldn't live where I wanted. Now what's the difference? **99**

Jesse Owens, US runner and long jumper, on racial discrimination during and after the Berlin Olympic Games, 1936.

Jesse Owens wins the Long Jump final at the Berlin Olympics.
10th July, 1936

"Whenever I saw Wally Hammond batting, I felt sorry for the ball. **"**

Len Hutton, on Wally Hammond, English cricketer, the best batsman in English cricket during the 1930s, scorer of a record 22 Test centuries.

England captain Wally Hammond (L) in conversation with the Australia captain, Lindsay Hassett, before the start of play for the Third Victory Test at Lord's cricket ground.
14th July, 1945

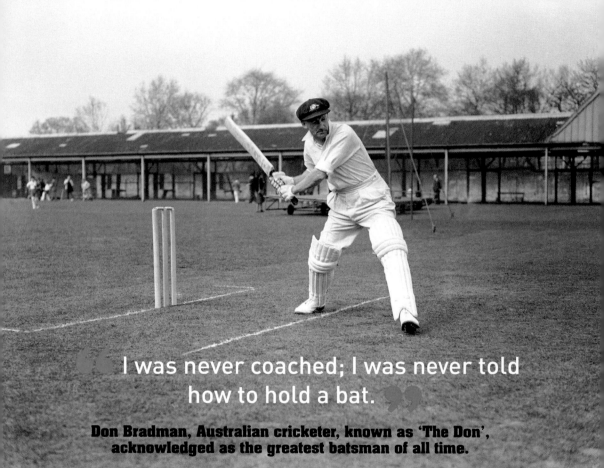

" I was never coached; I was never told how to hold a bat. **"**

Don Bradman, Australian cricketer, known as 'The Don', acknowledged as the greatest batsman of all time.

Australia's Don Bradman displays his batting prowess during a farewell tour of England before retiring from the game.
21st April, 1948

66 You can't climb up to the second floor without a ladder. When you set your aim too high and don't fulfil it, then your enthusiasm turns to bitterness. Try for a goal that's reasonable, and then gradually raise it. 99

Emil Zátopek, Czech long-distance runner and winner of three gold medals at the 1952 Helsinki Olympic Games.

Czechoslovakia's Emil Zátopek breaks the tape to win gold in the Men's 10,000m final at the London Olympic Games, Wembley.
30th July, 1948

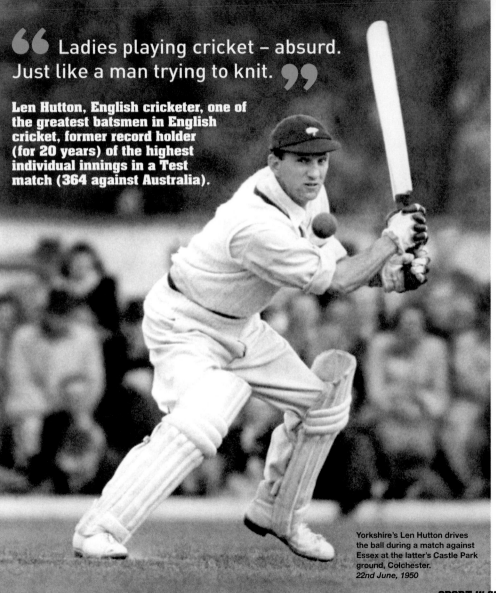

66 Ladies playing cricket – absurd. Just like a man trying to knit. 99

Len Hutton, English cricketer, one of the greatest batsmen in English cricket, former record holder (for 20 years) of the highest individual innings in a Test match (364 against Australia).

Yorkshire's Len Hutton drives the ball during a match against Essex at the latter's Castle Park ground, Colchester.
22nd June, 1950

> 66 I'll stay in football. I don't mind
> if they stand me up and use me
> as a corner flag. 99

Derek Dooley, English football player, manager and chairman, whose promising playing career was cut short when his infected right leg was amputated after he had fractured it badly during a match for Sheffield Wednesday.

Derek Dooley, of Sheffield Wednesday, and his wife wait to be taken home in an ambulance from Preston Royal Infirmary, after his leg had been amputated following a gangrene infection caused by him breaking the leg in a match against Preston North End.
6th April, 1953

> I'm no hero. Doctors and nurses are heroes. Surgeons, people like that. We had a real hero born right here in Stoke-on-Trent: Reginald Mitchell, who designed the Spitfire. He saved Britain. Now that's what I call a hero.

Stanley Matthews, English footballer, known as the 'Wizard of the Dribble', who played at the top level until the age of 50 and made 54 appearances for the national team, one of the greatest players of the English game.

Blackpool's Stanley Matthews (L) coolly steers the ball past Bolton's Malcolm Barrass during a thrilling FA Cup final at the Empire Stadium, Wembley. Matthews would go on to set up the fourth and winning goal by Bill Perry, giving Blackpool the Cup.
2nd May, 1953

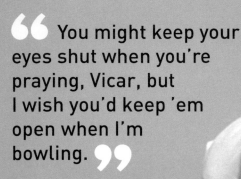

❝ You might keep your eyes shut when you're praying, Vicar, but I wish you'd keep 'em open when I'm bowling. **❞**

Fred Trueman, English cricketer, after the Rev. David Sheppard had dropped a catch off his bowling. Trueman appeared for England in 67 Test matches, the first bowler to take 300 wickets in a Test career, one of the greatest fast bowlers in the history of cricket.

'Fiery Fred' Trueman, England and Yorkshire fast bowler, demonstrates his powerful style at his club's Headingley ground in Leeds.
2nd May, 1953

66 Mother always told me my day was coming, but I never realized I'd end up being the shortest knight of the year. **99**

Gordon Richards, English jockey, considered by many to be the greatest jockey ever, and the only jockey to have been knighted.

Champion jockey Gordon Richards with his wife (R) and daughter outside Buckingham Palace, London, just before receiving his knighthood.
30th June, 1953

Roger Bannister, a 25-year-old medical student, hits the tape at an athletics meeting at Oxford to complete the world's first sub-four-minute mile (3 minutes 59.4 seconds).
6th May, 1954

66 Doctors and scientists said that breaking the four-minute mile was impossible, that one would die in the attempt. Thus, when I got up from the track after collapsing at the finish line, I figured I was dead. 99

Roger Bannister, English runner, first athlete to run the mile in under four minutes.

To boast of a performance which I cannot beat is merely stupid vanity. And if I can beat it that means there is nothing special about it. What has passed is already finished with. What I find more interesting is what is still to come.

Emil Zátopek, Czech long-distance runner and winner of three gold medals at the 1952 Helsinki Olympic Games.

Czech long-distance runner Emil Zátopek sets a new 5000m world record at the Colombes Stadium in Paris, France.
31st May, 1954

❝ There was plenty of fellers who would kick your bollocks off. The difference was that at the end they'd shake your hand and help you look for them. ❞

Nat Lofthouse, English footballer; played 33 times in the English national team.

England's Nat Lofthouse (R) wins a header during a World Cup match against Belgium in Switzerland.
17th June, 1954

"" To achieve anything in this game, you must be prepared to dabble on the boundary of disaster. ""

Stirling Moss, English racing driver, the greatest driver never to have won the World Championship.

Stirling Moss at the wheel of his Maserati during the RAC British Grand Prix at Silverstone; he would be forced to retire with a damaged rear axle.
12th July, 1954

“ A jump jockey has to throw his heart over the fence – and then go over and catch it. ”

Dick Francis, English jockey, racing correspondent and author.

Lochroe, ridden by Dick Francis, clears a hurdle during a race at Hurst Park, West Molesey, Surrey.
21st October, 1954

66 The greatest stimulator of my running career was fear. **99**

Herb Elliott, Australian runner who never lost a race over 1500m or the mile.

Australia's Herb Elliott crosses the line to win gold in the Mile at the British Empire and Commonwealth Games, Cardiff.
27th July, 1958

L–R: Jean Metcalfe, Brian Johnston, Wynford Vaughn-Thomas, Richard Dimbleby and Peter Dimmock, the team of BBC commentators for the forthcoming wedding of Princess Margaret and Anthony Armstrong-Jones.
30th April, 1960

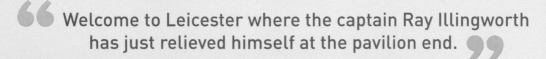

" Welcome to Leicester where the captain Ray Illingworth has just relieved himself at the pavilion end. "

Brian Johnston, English cricket commentator and broadcaster, known as 'Johnners', renowned for his humorous comments and gaffes.

66 Some people tell me that we professional players are soccer slaves. Well, if this is slavery, give me a life sentence. **99**

Bobby Charlton, English footballer who made 106 appearances for England at the highest level.

Bobby Charlton during a training session at Manchester United's Old Trafford ground. *3rd October, 1960*

66 I was taught that everything
is attainable if you
are prepared to give up,
to sacrifice, to get it. Whatever
you want to do, you can do it, if you want
it badly enough, and I do believe that.
I believe that if I wanted to run a mile
in four minutes I could do it. I would
have to give up everything else
in my life, but I could run a
mile in four minutes.
I believe that if a
man wanted to
walk on water
and was prepared to
give up everything else in
life, he could do that. **99**

**Stirling Moss, English racing driver, the greatest driver
never to have won the World Championship.**

Stirling Moss is the centre of attention as he holds the trophy for his victory in the 200-mile Silver City Trophy race at Brands Hatch in Kent. During the race, he lapped all but the next two finishers.
Brands Hatch, Kent.
3rd June, 1961

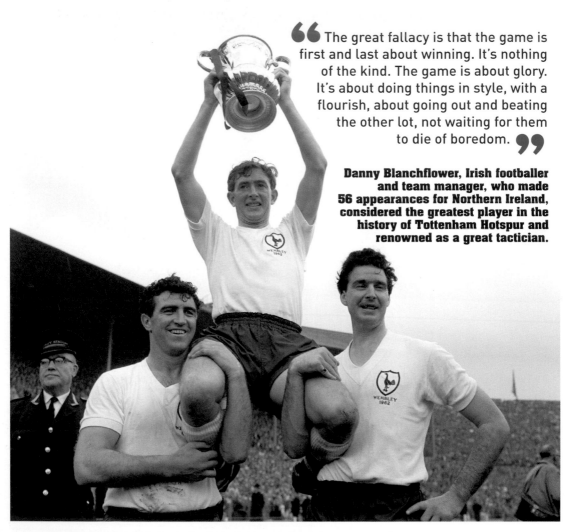

66 The great fallacy is that the game is first and last about winning. It's nothing of the kind. The game is about glory. It's about doing things in style, with a flourish, about going out and beating the other lot, not waiting for them to die of boredom. **99**

Danny Blanchflower, Irish footballer and team manager, who made 56 appearances for Northern Ireland, considered the greatest player in the history of Tottenham Hotspur and renowned as a great tactician.

Tottenham Hotspur's captain, Danny Blanchflower, holds the FA Cup aloft, after his team's 3–1 victory over Burnley at Wembley. Chairing Blanchflower are Bobby Smith (L) and Maurice Norman.
5th May, 1962

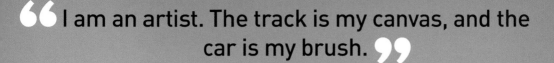

“ I am an artist. The track is my canvas, and the car is my brush. ”

Graham Hill, English racing driver, twice Formula 1 World Champion, winner of the Indianapolis 500 and Le Mans 24-hour race.

British Formula 1 racing driver Graham Hill, who had won the World Championship in 1962 and would take the crown again in 1968. *1st June, 1963*

Muhammad Ali during training
for his World Heavyweight
Championship fight
against Britain's
Henry Cooper.
20th May, 1966

**" I'm so fast that last
night I turned off the
light switch in my
hotel room and was
in bed before the room
was dark. "**

**Muhammad Ali, US boxer, three
times World Heavyweight Champion,
considered one of the greatest
heavyweight boxers of all time.**

World Heavyweight Champion Muhammad Ali plays the
piano during a press conference before the fight with Henry
Cooper. He stopped playing when someone in the crowd
shouted, "Take your gloves off!".
20th May, 1966

**" Float like a butterfly,
sting like a bee. "**

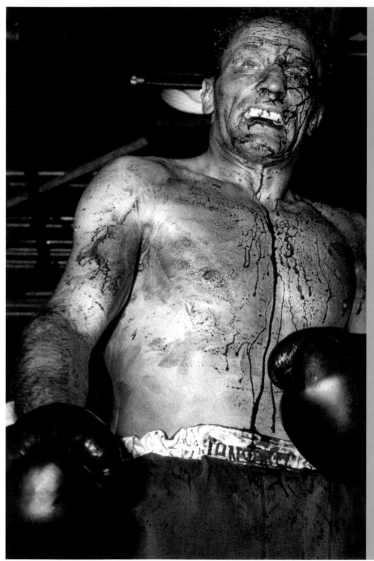

Blood pours from Henry Cooper's face as the referee stops the fight with Muhammad Ali in the sixth round at Highbury Stadium, London.
21st May, 1966

66 Mr Cooper, have you looked in the mirror lately and seen the state of your nose? 99

Boxing abolitionist Baroness Edith Summerskill.

66 Well madam, have you looked in the mirror and seen the state of your nose? Boxing is my excuse. What's yours? 99

Henry Cooper, English boxer, best known for knocking down a young Cassius Clay (Muhammad Ali) and defeating a number of well-known heavyweights.

> I've been asked about that goal every day for the last 40 years. We didn't have the technology back then to show whether it was a goal or not, which led to the controversy. I'd like to think one day we'll have the technology to show whether or not it was a goal.

Bobby Charlton, English footballer who made 106 appearances for England at the highest level.

Bobby Charlton (C) celebrates England's controversial third goal in the World Cup final, while West Germany's Wolfgang Weber (R) protests to the contrary. England would go on to win the match.
30th July, 1966

If you never concede a goal, you're going to win more games than you lose. 99

Bobby Moore, English footballer, captain of the England team that won the World Cup in 1966, who made 106 appearances for the national team, captain of West Ham United for over 10 years, one of the greatest players ever.

England's triumphant captain, Bobby Moore, is chaired by hat-trick hero Geoff Hurst (L) and Ray Wilson as he salutes the crowd with the Jules Rimet Trophy after the memorable 4–2 World Cup final victory over West Germany at Wembley.
30th July, 1966

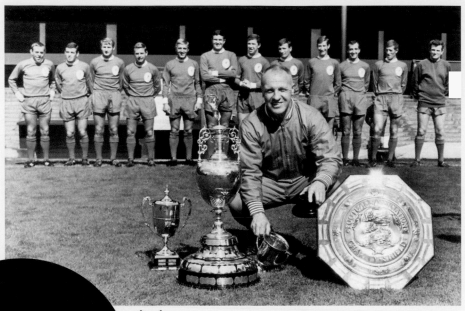

Liverpool manager Bill Shankly and his team with the trophies that they had won during the previous season, including the League Championship trophy and the FA Charity Shield.
15th August, 1966

Liverpool manager Bill Shankly in characteristic pose.
1st August, 1966

> 66 If you're not sure what to do with the ball, just pop it in the net and we'll discuss your options afterwards. 99

Bill Shankly, Scottish footballer and manager, best known for his achievements with Liverpool, who became a major force in the English game under his management.

> 66 Some people think football is a matter of life and death. I assure you, it's much more serious than that. 99

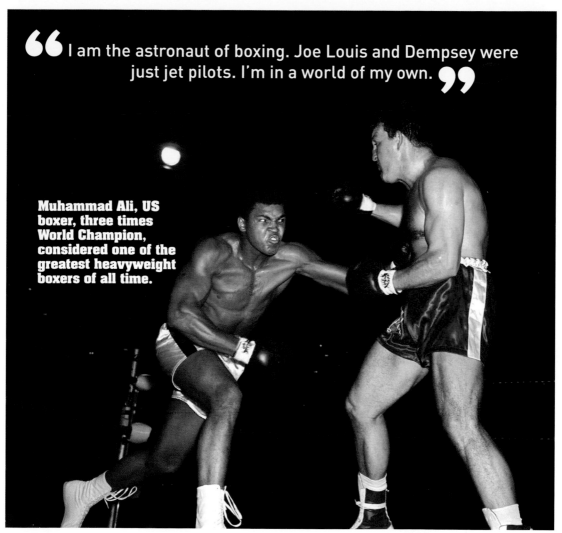

66 I am the astronaut of boxing. Joe Louis and Dempsey were just jet pilots. I'm in a world of my own. **99**

Muhammad Ali, US boxer, three times World Champion, considered one of the greatest heavyweight boxers of all time.

Muhammad Ali (L) catches Brian London with a left to the gut during a World Heavyweight title fight at Earls Court, London. The English boxer was no match for 'The Louisville Lip', who made short work of his opponent.
6th August, 1966

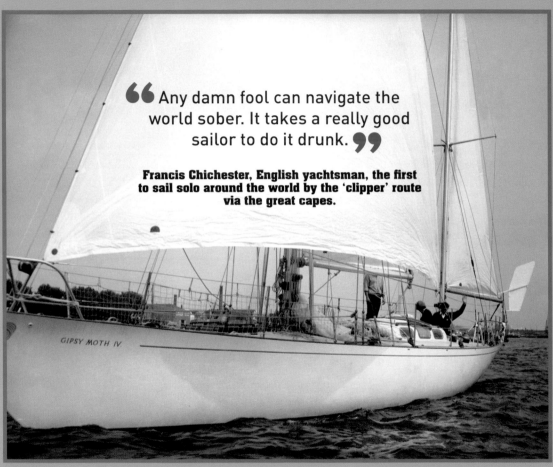

66 Any damn fool can navigate the world sober. It takes a really good sailor to do it drunk. **99**

Francis Chichester, English yachtsman, the first to sail solo around the world by the 'clipper' route via the great capes.

Francis Chichester (R) waves to photographers before setting off from Plymouth, Devon, on his solo around-the-world voyage in *Gipsy Moth IV*. *15th August, 1966*

Nottingham Forest goalkeeper Peter Grummitt (L) saves from a header by Tottenham Hotspur's Jimmy Greaves (C), watched by team-mates (L–R) Henry Newton, Peter Hindley, Terry Hennessey (hidden), John Winfield and Bob McKinlay. 29th April, 1967

"He was the Fagin of the penalty area, the arch-pickpocket of goals."

Geoffrey Green, football writer, on Jimmy Greaves.

"It was a very simple team talk. All I used to say was, 'Whenever possible, give the ball to George'."

Matt Busby, Manchester United manager, on George Best, who spent 11 years with the team, from 1963 to 1974.

Manchester United's George Best in action. Best was elected Footballer of the Year in 1968 by the members of the Football Writers' Association. He polled 60 per cent of the votes to become, at 21, the youngest player ever to receive the honour.
1968

66 I would have been a much more popular World Champion if I had always said what people wanted to hear. I might have been dead, but definitely more popular. 99

Jackie Stewart, Scottish racing driver and team owner, three-times Formula 1 World Champion.

"It was much easier 38 years ago, no messing around with technology. They said I was missing for four-and-a-half months and prepared my obituary, but I always knew where I was."

Robin Knox-Johnston, English yachtsman, the first to complete a solo, non-stop circumnavigation of the world.

> **These greens are so fast I have to hold my putter over the ball and hit it with the shadow.**

Sam Snead, US golfer, known as 'Slammin' Sammy', winner of 82 PGA Tour events.

The two captains, Sam Snead of the United States (L) and Eric Brown of Britain, exchange the names of their teams prior to the opening of play in the Ryder Cup golf tournament at Royal Birkdale, Southport, Lancashire.
16th September, 1969

At Beaulieu in Hampshire, Sir Francis Chichester prepares his new yacht, *Gipsy Moth V*, for his 200-miles-a-day, 4,000-mile voyage from Bissau, Portuguese Guinea, to Juan del Norte, Nicaragua.
1st December, 1970

66 To the question, 'When were your spirits at the lowest ebb?' the obvious answer seemed to be, 'When the gin gave out.'**99**

Francis Chichester, English yachtsman, the first to sail solo around the world by the 'clipper' route via the great capes.

" Nobby Stiles a dirty player? No, he's never hurt anyone. Mind you, he's frightened a few! **"**

Matt Busby, manager of Manchester United from 1945 to 1969 and part of the 1970/71 season, on English player Nobby Stiles, who spent 11 years with the club and was a member of England's victorious World Cup team in 1966.

Nobby Stiles, of Manchester United, reties his laces prior to a match against Chelsea.
9th January, 1971

Stoke City goalkeeper Gordon Banks shows off his greatest assets at the Britannia Stadium, Stoke-on-Trent. *30th April, 1971*

" That save from Pelé's header was the best I ever made. I didn't have any idea how famous it would become – to start with, I didn't even realize I'd made it at all. "

Gordon Banks, English goalkeeper, on his incredible save against Pelé during the 1970 World Cup in Mexico.

Rod Laver in action during the Wimbledon
Men's Singles quarter final against Tom Gorman.
28th June, 1971

" I often surprise myself. You can't plan
some shots that go in, not unless you're
on marijuana, and the only grass I'm
partial to is Wimbledon's. "

**Rod Laver, Australian tennis player, former
World Number One, the only tennis player to
have won all four Grand Slam titles in the same
year twice.**

66 Running is a lot like life. Only 10 per cent of it is exciting; 90 per cent of it is slog and drudge. **99**

David Bedford, English long-distance runner, holder of the world record for the 10,000m in 1973.

A determined David Bedford takes part in an Invitation cross-country race over an 8,000m course at Parliament Fields, Hampstead, London, which he won.
27th November, 1971

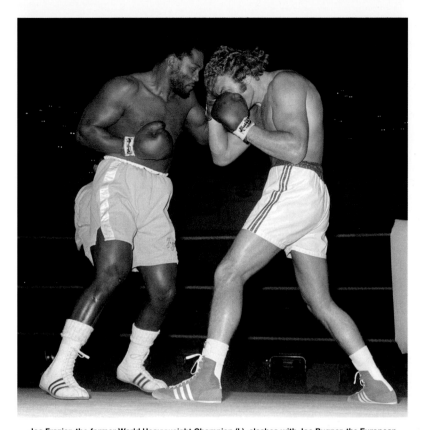

Joe Frazier, the former World Heavyweight Champion (L), clashes with Joe Bugner, the European Champion, during a 12-round bout at Earls Court, London. Frazier was the victor.
2nd July, 1973

Boxing is the only sport you can get your brain shook, your money took and your name in the undertaker book.

Joe Frazier, US boxer known as 'Smokin' Joe', Olympic gold medallist and former World Heavyweight champion.

> ❝ You can't catch a 'coon with your dog tied up. ❞

Alfred 'Rabbit' Dyer, caddie, to South African golfer Gary Player, when he saw that Player was nervous and holding back on his shots during the 1974 British Open; Player went on to win the event.

South African Gary Player (R), at Royal Lytham & St Annes, Lancashire, for the British Open Golf Championship, with his American caddie, Alfred 'Rabbit' Dyer. Player would go on to win the event, his eighth major championship victory.
8th July, 1974

66 I don't care who you are, you're going to choke in certain matches. You get to a point where your legs don't move and you can't take a deep breath. You start to hit the ball about a yard wide, instead of inches. 99

Arthur Ashe, US tennis player, winner of three Grand Slam men's singles titles.

US player Arthur Ashe in action on the Centre Court at Wimbledon, during his quarter-final clash with Sweden's Björn Borg. Ashe would triumph and go on to win the final.
1st July, 1975

US tennis player Billie-Jean King in action during her Wimbledon Women's Singles final match against Evonne Cawley of Australia. King became champion for the sixth time after beating Cawley 6–0 6–1.
4th July, 1975

Billie-Jean King, US tennis player, winner of 12 Grand Slam singles titles and 11 Grand Slam mixed doubles titles.

66 Tennis is a perfect combination of violent action taking place in an atmosphere of total tranquility. 99

66 There is no path I follow. I feel as if I'm just drifting along, because although I can progress physically through my training, mentally and spiritually I don't know what the hell I'm doing. It's like that car sticker: 'Don't follow me, I'm lost.' 99

Steve Ovett, English middle-distance runner, 800m gold medallist at the 1980 Moscow Olympic Games.

66 You don't run 26 miles at five minutes a mile on good looks and a secret recipe. **99**

Frank Shorter, US long-distance runner, Marathon gold medallist at the 1972 Munich Olympic Games.

The USA's Frank Shorter enters the stadium to finish the Marathon in silver-medal position at the Montreal Olympic Games, Canada.
1st August, 1976

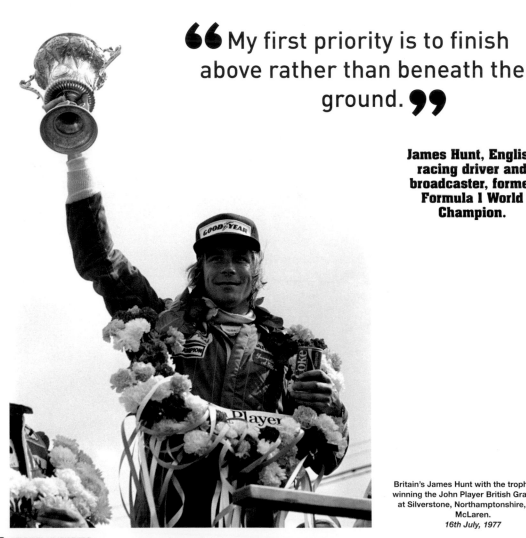

66 My first priority is to finish above rather than beneath the ground. **99**

James Hunt, English racing driver and broadcaster, former Formula 1 World Champion.

Britain's James Hunt with the trophy after winning the John Player British Grand Prix at Silverstone, Northamptonshire, in his McLaren.
16th July, 1977

Playing for New York Cosmos late in his career, Pelé takes the ball as team-mates Franz Beckenbauer and Carlos Alberto look on during a SoccerBowl '77 match against the Seattle Sounders at Portland's Civic Stadium in Oregon. New York won the match 2–1.
28th August, 1977

❛ A penalty is a cowardly way to score. ❜❜

Pelé, Brazilian footballer, one of the greatest players of all time.

Muhammad Ali, 'The Louisville Lip', in full flow. A few weeks after this photograph was taken, he would defeat Leon Spinks and regain the World Heavyweight title for the third time.
10th August, 1978

66 Musically speaking, if Larry Holmes don't C sharp, he'll B flat. **99**

Muhammad Ali, US boxer, three times World Champion, considered one of the greatest heavyweight boxers.

❝ Sure there have been injuries and deaths in boxing – but none of them serious. **❞**

Alan Minter, English middleweight boxer, former ABA Middleweight Champion, bronze medallist at the 1972 Munich Olympic Games, winner of 39 fights, 23 by KO.

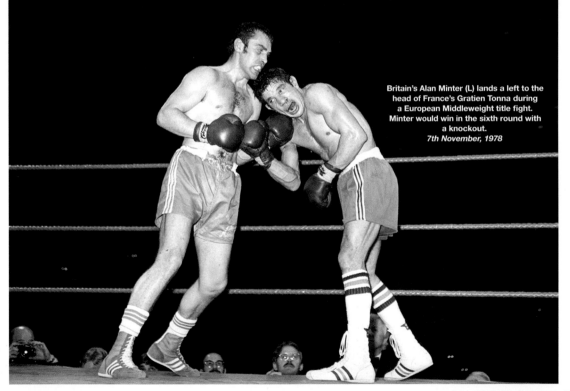

Britain's Alan Minter (L) lands a left to the head of France's Gratien Tonna during a European Middleweight title fight. Minter would win in the sixth round with a knockout.
7th November, 1978

Kevin Keegan in action for
Hamburg during a Bundesliga
game in Germany.
28th March, 1979

66 Football's
always
easier when
you've got the
ball. **99**

**Kevin Keegan, English footballer and
team manager who made 63 appearances
for England.**

> 66 I don't run away from a challenge because I am afraid. Instead, I run toward it because the only way to escape fear is to trample it beneath your feet. 99

Nadia Comaneci, Romanian gymnast, winner of three gold medals at the 1976 Montreal Olympic Games and two gold medals at the 1980 Moscow Olympic Games.

Romanian gymnast Nadia Comaneci, the World and Olympic Beam Champion, limbers up at Wembley Arena in preparation for the *Daily Mirror* Champions All international gymnastics tournament.
6th April, 1979

Continental Sports

66 *My basic problem was that I would get all tripped out by the negatives – bad calls, bad days, bad feelings – and anger got to be a habit. I was like a compulsive gambler or an alcoholic. Anger became a powerful habit.* 99

John McEnroe, US tennis player, former World Number One, winner of seven Grand Slam men's singles titles, nine Grand Slam men's doubles titles and one Grand Slam mixed doubles title; well known for his confrontational manner on court; one of the greatest male tennis players of all time.

66 My greatest point is my persistence. I never give up in a match. However down I am, I fight until the last ball. My list of matches shows that I have turned a great many so-called irretrievable defeats into victories. 99

Björn Borg, Swedish tennis player, former World Number One, winner of 11 Grand Slam men's singles titles and five consecutive Wimbledon singles titles, one of the greatest male tennis players of all time.

Sweden's Björn Borg sinks to his knees on the Centre Court at the All England Club, Wimbledon after winning his fifth successive Men's Singles title with a thrilling five-sets victory over 21-year-old American John McEnroe.
5th July, 1980

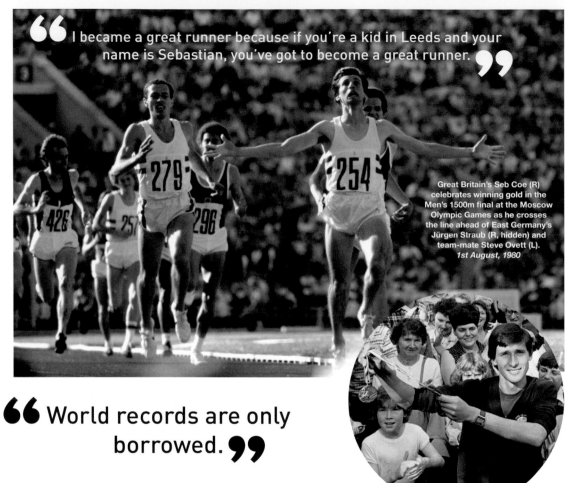

> **I became a great runner because if you're a kid in Leeds and your name is Sebastian, you've got to become a great runner.**

Great Britain's Seb Coe (R) celebrates winning gold in the Men's 1500m final at the Moscow Olympic Games as he crosses the line ahead of East Germany's Jürgen Straub (R, hidden) and team-mate Steve Ovett (L).
1st August, 1980

> **World records are only borrowed.**

Sebastian Coe, English middle-distance runner and chairman of the organizing committee for the 2012 London Olympic Games, winner of four gold medals at the Olympic Games of 1980 and 1984.

Sebastian Coe, the 1500m Olympic Champion, proudly shows off his medals to friends and family outside his Sheffield home after returning from the Moscow Olympic Games. Coe won gold in the 1500m and silver in the 800m.
3rd August, 1980

Australian captain Greg Chappell steers a delivery from his opposite number, Ian Botham, through the England slips at Lord's Cricket Ground, St John's Wood, London, during the first day's play in the Centenary Test match.
28th August, 1980

❝ I can't really say I'm batting badly. I'm not batting long enough to be batting badly. ❞

Greg Chappell, Australian cricketer, captain of Australia between 1975 and 1977, and 1979 and 1983, who played in 87 Test matches; an exceptional all-rounder.

66 Alan Butcher drops his head, both hands behind his back and looks sheepishly down the wicket like a small boy caught stealing jam. **99**

John Arlott, cricket commentator, known for his poetic style of delivery, on Surrey and Glamorgan player Alan Butcher.

BBC Radio commentator John Arlott at Lord's Cricket Ground, St John's Wood, London, during the last day of his final commentary, which covered the Centenary Test match between England and Australia.
2nd September, 1980

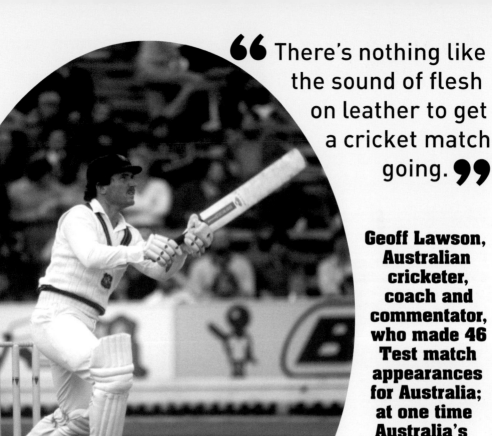

❝ There's nothing like the sound of flesh on leather to get a cricket match going. **❞**

Geoff Lawson, Australian cricketer, coach and commentator, who made 46 Test match appearances for Australia; at one time Australia's leading fast bowler.

Geoff Lawson, batting for Australia and on his way to making 29 not out during the Second One Day International between England and Australia, at Edgbaston, Birmingham.
6th June, 1981

Darts player Eric Bristow, 'The Crafty Cockney', demonstrates his throwing technique, with "perked up right pinkie".
1st July, 1981

66 Bristow reasons;
Bristow quickens;
Aaaaah Bristow! 99

Sid Waddell, sports commentator, on Eric Bristow, English darts player, known as 'The Crafty Cockney', the most successful and consistent darts player of the 1980s, five times winner of the BDO World Darts Championship.

John McEnroe (L) confronts Jimmy Connors at the net during a tempestuous singles final at the Benson & Hedges Championships, Wembley. *18th November, 1981*

❝ I don't know that my behaviour has improved that much with age. They just found someone worse. **❞**

Jimmy Connors, US tennis player, former World Number One, winner of eight Grand Slam men's singles titles and two Grand Slam men's doubles titles, on John McEnroe.

" Tee the ball high. Because years of experience have shown me that air offers less resistance to dirt. **"**

Jack Nicklaus, US golfer known as 'The Golden Bear', winner of 18 major championships, one of the greatest professional golfers of all time.

American Jack Nicklaus drives off in front of a rapt audience.
1982

"I'm short and fat. So what? That's life! Anyway, TV makes you look fatter."

Jocky Wilson, Scottish darts player, two times World Professional Darts Champion, four times winner of the British Professional Darts Championship.

Scotland's Jocky Wilson, from Kirkaldy, Fife, on the day after he had beaten John Lowe in the final of the Embassy World Professional Darts Championship at Jollees Cabaret Club, Stoke-on-Trent, to take the title and the £6,500 first prize.
17th January, 1982

66 A boxer makes a comeback for two reasons: either he's broke or he needs the money. **99**

Alan Minter, English middleweight boxer, former ABA Middleweight Champion, bronze medallist at the 1972 Munich Olympic Games, winner of 39 fights, 23 by KO.

Former World Middleweight Champion Alan Minter lines up a new challenger – his own waxwork, on show at Selfridge's store in London's Oxford Street.
28th June, 1982

66 Diego Maradona – a flawed genius who has now become a genius who is flawed. **99**

Bob Wilson, former goalkeeper and football commentator, on Argentine player Diego Maradona, who made 91 appearances for his national team and is considered by many to be one of the greatest footballers of all time; drug problems proved his undoing.

Argentina's Diego Maradona (L) gets away from Brazil's Leandro during a World Cup Group C match at the Sarria Stadium in Spain.
2nd July, 1982

Old England's Fred Trueman (L) shares a bottle of champagne with Old World XI's Garry Sobers after their match at the Oval cricket ground, south London.
19th September, 1982

66 You can't consider yourself a county cricketer until you've eaten half a ton of lettuce. 99

Garry Sobers, West Indies cricketer, one of the game's greatest all-rounders, an excellent batsman, bowler and fielder, who appeared in 93 Test matches for West Indies and who played for Nottinghamshire between 1968 and 1974.

Manchester United manager Ron Atkinson with his partner, Maggie Harrison, at a press conference in Altrincham, Greater Manchester. *12th May, 1984*

> **Women should be in the kitchen, the discotheque and the boutique, but not in football.**

Ron Atkinson, English football player, manager and television pundit, known as 'Big Ron'; well known for his unique turn of phrase.

66 Being a decathlete is like having ten girlfriends. You have to love them all, and you can't afford losing one. **99**

Daley Thompson, English decathlete, gold medallist at the 1980 Moscow Olympic Games and 1984 Los Angeles Olympic Games, four times world record holder for the decathlon, considered by many to be the greatest decathlete of all time.

Great Britain's Daley Thompson putting the shot as part of the Decathlon during the Los Angeles Olympic Games. He would win gold in the event.
8th August, 1984

66 You can't drink too many otherwise you can't see what you're throwing at. **99**

Eric Bristow, English darts player, known as 'The Crafty Cockney', the most successful and consistent darts player of the 1980s, five times winner of the BDO World Darts Championship.

Eric Bristow with the trophy after winning the World Professional Darts Championship final against John Lowe at Jollees Cabaret Club, Stoke-on-Trent.
13th January, 1985

A victorious Barry McGuigan holds his gloved hands aloft in celebration after winning the WBA Featherweight title fight against Panama's Eusebio Pedroza (inset) at Queens Park Rangers football ground, Shepherd's Bush, London.
8th June, 1985

66 It is not the size of the dog in the fight that counts, but the size of the fight in the dog. 99

Barry McGuigan, Irish boxer, former World Featherweight champion.

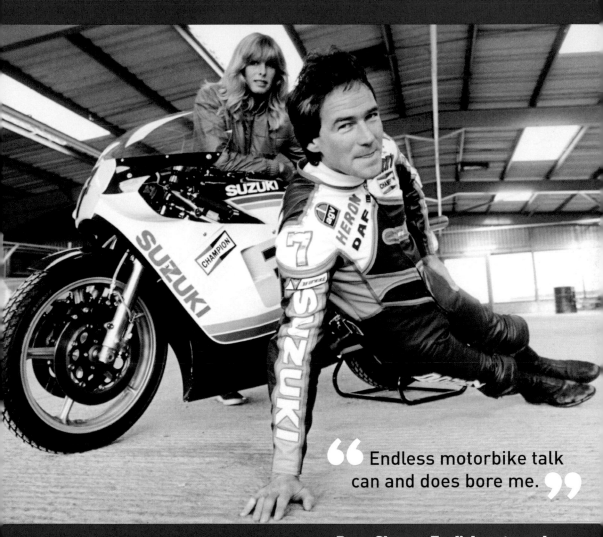

British motorcycle racer Barry Sheene demonstrates his strength while his wife Stephanie looks on. Sheene's many racing injuries caused him to develop arthritis, and in an attempt to relieve the pain he moved to a warmer climate in Australia. 1st July, 1985.

66 Endless motorbike talk can and does bore me. 99

Barry Sheene, English motorcycle racer and broadcaster, former Grand Prix World Champion.

Tottenham Hotspur's signing from Newcastle, Chris Waddle (second R), tries to find a way through three of his former team-mates in a First Division clash at White Hart Lane, London.
8th September, 1985

My legs sort of disappeared from nowhere.

Chris Waddle, English footballer and commentator, who made 62 appearances for England.

" Man, it don't matter where you come in to bat, the score is still zero. **"**

Viv Richards, West Indies cricketer, who appeared in 121 Test matches for West Indies, third greatest Test batsman of all time, scorer of 8,540 Test match runs.

Somerset's Viv Richards (R) with Jon Hardy batting in a NatWest Trophy match against Lancashire. *9th July, 1986*

Frank Bruno (R) and WBA World Heavyweight Champion Tim Witherspoon land punches simultaneously during a World Heavyweight title fight at Wembley Stadium. Witherspoon of Philadelphia, USA, retained his title after the referee stopped the fight in the 11th round.
20th July, 1986

❝ Since I didn't want to go round mugging old ladies or robbing banks, I took up boxing. **❞**

Frank Bruno, English boxer, former WBC Heavyweight champion, winner of 40 of his 45 contests, on why he became a boxer.

Transatlantic yachtsmen Chay Blyth and Richard Branson take the helm of *Cutty Sark* at Greenwich, London, to launch their latest venture – British Clippers – a scheme that involved the conversion of two coasters into 19th-century clippers, which would tour the coast of America and Canada during 1988 and 1989 to boost trade and tourism from the USA to Britain.
16th September, 1986

 Seize the opportunity of a lifetime in the lifetime of the opportunity.

Chay Blyth, Scottish yachtsman and transoceanic rower, the first person to sail non-stop westward around the world.

BBC Radio Four's Brian Johnston (R) fools around with cricket legend Denis Compton to commemorate the last ever edition of Johnston's programme *Down Your Way*.
20th May, 1987

" As he comes into bowl, Freddie Titmus has got two short legs, one of them square. **"**

Brian Johnston, English cricket commentator and broadcaster, known as 'Johnners', renowned for his humorous comments and gaffes.

> 66 I don't psyche myself up. I psyche myself down. I think clearer when I'm not psyched up. 99

Steve Cauthen, US jockey, the first to win $6m in a single season (1977 - only his second year of riding), youngest jockey ever to win the US Triple Crown, three times British Champion Jockey, winner of 10 classic English races.

The Henry Cecil trained bay colt Reference Point is led into the winner's enclosure with American jockey Steve Cauthen aboard after winning the Derby at Epsom, Surrey. *3rd June, 1987*

Fred Trueman, English cricketer, on Ian Botham, English cricketer and commentator, known as 'Beefy', former England Test team captain who scored 14 centuries and took 383 wickets in Test cricket.

A determined Ian Botham batting for England during the first day of the Third Test match against Pakistan at Headingley. Leeds.
2nd July, 1987

66 The mark of great sportsmen is not how good they are at their best, but how good they are at their worst. **99**

Martina Navratilova, Czech/US tennis player, former World Number one, winner of 18 Grand Slam women's singles titles, 31 Grand Slam women's doubles titles and 10 Grand Slam mixed doubles titles.

Martina Navratilova celebrates victory over Steffi Graf in the Women's Singles final at the All England Club, Wimbledon.
4th July, 1987

66 Players lose you games, not tactics. There's so much crap talked about tactics by people who barely know how to win at dominoes. 99

Brian Clough, English footballer and team manager, remembered for being outspoken and often controversial, considered by many to be the greatest English manager never to have managed the English team; reflecting on England's exit from Euro 2000.

Nottingham Forest manager Brian Clough makes an unambiguous gesture during a League Division One match against Arsenal at the City Ground, Nottingham.
12th September, 1987

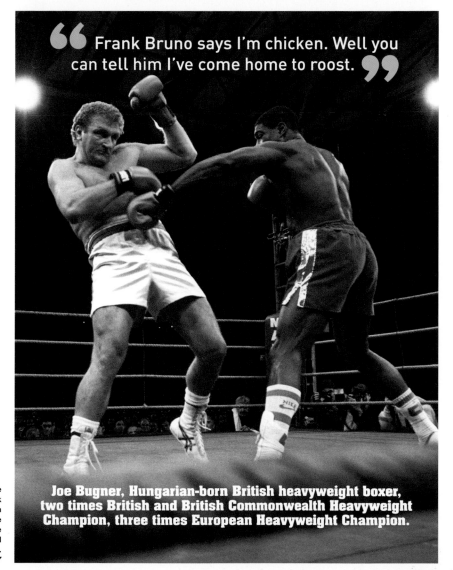

Frank Bruno says I'm chicken. Well you can tell him I've come home to roost.

Joe Bugner (L) takes the brunt of a left jab from Frank Bruno, who would go on to win the bout at White Hart Lane, London, in the eighth round with a technical knockout.
24th October, 1987

Joe Bugner, Hungarian-born British heavyweight boxer, two times British and British Commonwealth Heavyweight Champion, three times European Heavyweight Champion.

" Mary Decker Slaney, the world's greatest front-runner; I shouldn't be surprised to see her at the front. **"**

Ron Pickering, television sports commentator, on Mary Decker Slaney, US middle-distance runner, 1500m and 3000m gold medallist at the 1983 Helsinki World Championships.

Yvonne Murray of Great Britain (L) runs with Mary Decker-Slaney of the USA during the Women's 3000m race at the Seoul Olympic Games, South Korea. Murray won the bronze medal.
25th September, 1988

Great Britain's Fatima Whitbread launches the javelin, on her way to winning the silver medal during the Seoul Olympic Games in South Korea.
29th September, 1988

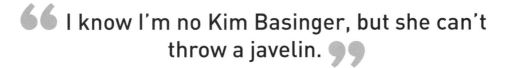

66 I know I'm no Kim Basinger, but she can't throw a javelin. 99

Fatima Whitbread, English javelin thrower, former world champion, bronze and silver medallist respectively at the 1984 Los Angelis and 1988 Seoul Olympic Games.

Tributes laid at Anfield football ground, home of Liverpool Football Club, in memory of those who died in the Hillsborough disaster, Sheffield, during an FA Cup semi-final match between Liverpool and Nottingham Forest.
17th April, 1989

❝ The saddest and most beautiful sight I have ever seen. ❞

Kenny Dalglish, English footballer, on scarves left in tribute at Anfield by Liverpool fans following the Hillsborough disaster, when 96 Liverpool supporters died and 766 were injured at the Sheffield Wednesday ground after a crowd surge caused a crush.

L–R: Former World Heavyweight champions Joe Frazier, George Foreman and Muhammad Ali publicize the launch of the video *Champions Forever*, a tribute to their fight careers.
17th October, 1989

66 I've seen George Foreman shadow boxing and the shadow won. 99

Muhammad Ali, on George Foreman, US heavyweight boxer two times World Heavyweight Champion, heavyweight boxing gold medallist at the 1968 Mexico City Olympic Games, one of the hardest hitters in boxing history.

66 We signed to play until the day we died, and we did. **99**

Jimmy Greaves, English footballer and television pundit, who made 57 appearances for England, England's third highest international goal scorer, highest goal scorer in the history of English top-level football, known for his catchphrase: "It's a funny old game."

Football pundits and former players Ian St John (L) and Jimmy Greaves get in the mood for the 1990 World Cup in Rome.
8th December, 1989

> **"** Desert Orchid can't say he's as 'sick as a parrot', or that he won't be quoted until you've talked to his agent. As a gelding, he's unlikely to make the nookie sections of the tabloids. He just sets off towards the fences and invites you to throw your spirit with him. **"**

Brough Scott, racing commentator, 1989.

Equine superstar Desert Orchid, at home in north Yorkshire, receives a peck from owner Richard Burridge before the cameras – rolling for the horse's own television show.
8th December, 1989

" If I am still standing at the end of the race, hit me with a board and knock me down, because that means I didn't run hard enough. "

Steve Jones, Welsh long-distance runner, former world record holder, 10,000m bronze medallist at the 1986 Commonwealth Games.

Former world record holder Steve Jones, from Wales, competing in the Marathon at the Commonwealth Games in Auckland, New Zealand, where he would finish in fourth place.
1990

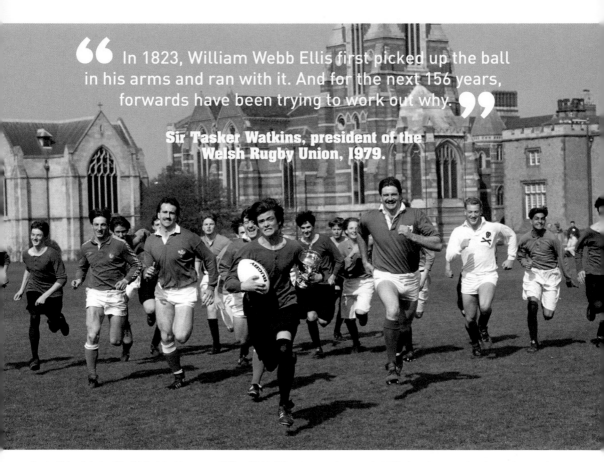

> " In 1823, William Webb Ellis first picked up the ball in his arms and ran with it. And for the next 156 years, forwards have been trying to work out why. "
>
> **Sir Tasker Watkins, president of the Welsh Rugby Union, 1979.**

Rugby School student Daniel Enright-Mooney, as William Webb Ellis, re-enacts the scene in 1823 when the game of rugby was born at the school in Warwickshire. He is being chased by international stars (L–R) Philippe Sella (France), Bob Norster (Wales), Robert Jones (Wales) and Willie Anderson (Ireland), and the rest of the school team.
27th March, 1990

> **"** Football is a simple game. Twenty-two men chase a ball for 90 minutes and at the end, the Germans always win. **"**

Gary Lineker, English footballer and sports broadcaster, appeared 80 times for England, becoming England's top goal scorer in the World Cup finals.

Gary Lineker scores in the penalty shoot-out during the World Cup semi-final between West Germany and England at the Stadio delle Alpi, Turin, Italy.
4th July, 1990

66 Chris Eubank arrives in the boxing ring posing and parading like a peacock, so risible that even his opponent and his opponent's corner men have to laugh ... a preposterous pugilist. 99

Michael Hard, writing in the *Evening Standard*, on Chris Eubank, English middleweight and super middleweight boxer, world champion for over five years.

Boxer Chris Eubank strikes a typically arrogant pose.
18th November, 1990

66 When I lost my decathlon world record, I took it like a man. I only cried for ten hours. **99**

Daley Thompson, English decathlete, gold medallist at the 1980 Moscow Olympic Games and 1984 Los Angeles Olympic Games, four times world record holder for the decathlon, considered by many to be the greatest decathlete of all time.

Great Britain's decathlete Daley Thompson expresses his feelings about his performance in the pole vault at Alhama de Murcia, Spain. He would retire from competition in the following year.
2nd June, 1991

66 We estimate, and this isn't an estimation, that Greta Waitz is 80 seconds behind. 99

David Coleman, English sports commentator, holder of the Olympic Order in recognition of his services to the Olympic ideals, known for his gaffes and nonsensical remarks on air.

BBC Television commentator David Coleman at work during the Europa Cup athletics event in Frankfurt.
29th June, 1991

66 Neil Harvey's at slip, with his legs wide apart, waiting for a tickle. **99**

Brian Johnston, English cricket commentator and broadcaster, known as 'Johnners', renowned for his humorous comments and gaffes.

Brian Johnston, veteran cricket commentator, wearing his lucky Test match shoes at Lord's Cricket Ground, St John's Wood, London. 'Johnners' was nearing his 80th birthday and still working, but he would suffer a fatal heart attack 18 months later.
17th June, 1992

Linford Christie of Great Britain wins gold in the Men's 100m final at the Barcelona Olympic Games.
1st August, 1992

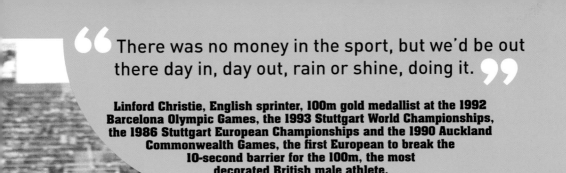

> **There was no money in the sport, but we'd be out there day in, day out, rain or shine, doing it.**

Linford Christie, English sprinter, 100m gold medallist at the 1992 Barcelona Olympic Games, the 1993 Stuttgart World Championships, the 1986 Stuttgart European Championships and the 1990 Auckland Commonwealth Games, the first European to break the 10-second barrier for the 100m, the most decorated British male athlete.

> **I hope to be the fastest fat old git in the race.**

Eamon Martin, English long-distance runner, winner of the 1993 London Marathon and 1995 Chicago Marathon.

London Marathon winner 35-year-old Eamonn Martin proudly holds aloft his trophy. Commonwealth 10,000m champion and Ford worker from Basildon, Essex, Martin was England's first winner in the famous event since 1984.
18th April, 1993

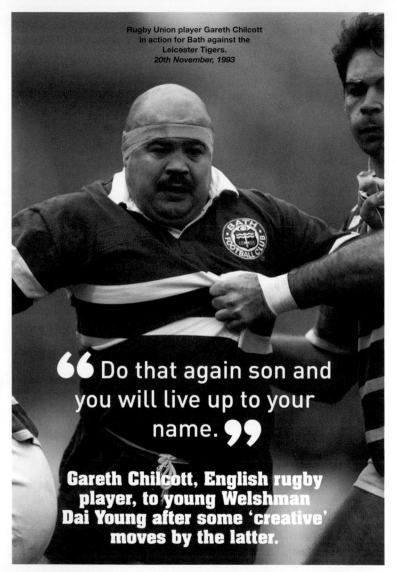

Rugby Union player Gareth Chilcott in action for Bath against the Leicester Tigers.
20th November, 1993

❝ Do that again son and you will live up to your name. ❞

Gareth Chilcott, English rugby player, to young Welshman Dai Young after some 'creative' moves by the latter.

Czech former runner Emil Zátopek and British javelin thrower Fatima Whitbread swap stories at lunch during the European Athletics Championship in Helsinki, Finland.
14th August, 1994

66 **An athlete cannot run with money in his pockets. He must run with hope in his heart and dreams in his head.** 99

Emil Zátopek, Czech long-distance runner and winner of three gold medals at the 1952 Helsinki Olympic Games.

Wimbledon's Vinnie Jones (R)
clashes with Scott Gemmill of
Nottingham Forest.
13th May, 1995

66 The FA have given me a pat on the back. I've taken violence off the terracing and on to the pitch. **99**

Vinnie Jones, English footballer and actor who captained the Welsh national team by virtue of having a Welsh grandparent, known for being a 'tough guy' on the pitch.

" We're going to tear those boys apart. "

Will Carling, English rugby player, message as captain to his team prior to the 1995 World Cup semi-final against New Zealand, which the All Blacks won 45–29.

Frank Bruno throws a left to the head of WBC Heavyweight Champion Oliver McCall in the first round of their title fight at Wembley Stadium. Bruno would win on points after 12 rounds.
2nd September, 1995

> **It was like a Michael Jackson concert, Pavarotti, Vera Lynn and VE Day, all rolled into one.**

Frank Bruno, English boxer, former WBC Heavyweight champion, winner of 40 of his 45 contests, on winning the world title fight in 1995.

Manchester United's Eric Cantona volleys in the equalizing goal against Sheffield Wednesday during a Carling **Premier** League match.
9th December, 1995

I'd give all the champagne I've ever drunk to have played alongside Eric Cantona in a big European match at Old Trafford.

George Best, on French footballer Eric Cantona, who spent five years at Manchester United, where Best had enjoyed his best years in the game.

Steffi Graf keeps a tight hold on the trophy after winning the Women's Singles title at the All England Club, Wimbledon.
6th July, 1996

66 When you lose a couple of times, it makes you realize how difficult it is to win. 99

Steffi Graf, German tennis player, former World Number One, winner of 22 Grand Slam women's singles titles, winner of all four Grand Slam events and an Olympic gold medal in the same year (1988).

66 It's only jumping into a sandpit. **99**

Jonathan Edwards, English triple jumper, Olympic gold medallist; former Commonwealth, European and World champion; world record holder.

Great Britain's Jonathan Edwards takes part in the Men's Triple Jump final during the Atlanta Olympic Games, USA. His effort would be rewarded with a silver medal.
27th July, 1996

Michael Johnson's gold Nike trainers, worn at the Atlanta Olympic Games, USA. 27th July, 1996

" They don't give you gold medals for beating somebody. They give you gold medals for beating everybody. "

Michael Johnson, American sprinter, winner of four Olympic gold medals, eight times world champion, the greatest long sprinter in history.

Great Britain's Roger Black finishes second behind the celebrating Michael Johnson in the 400m final at the Atlanta Olympic Games, USA.
29th July, 1996

66 Don't talk about Michael Johnson's style. Look, if that guy ran with his fingers up his bum, he could still run 42 seconds. **99**

Roger Black, English sprinter and broadcaster, on US sprinter Michael Johnson.

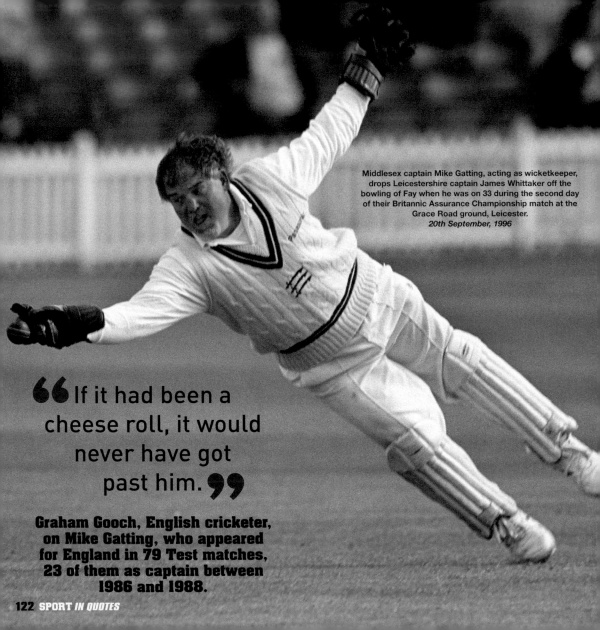

Middlesex captain Mike Gatting, acting as wicketkeeper,
drops Leicestershire captain James Whittaker off the
bowling of Fay when he was on 33 during the second day
of their Britannic Assurance Championship match at the
Grace Road ground, Leicester.
20th September, 1996

66 If it had been a
cheese roll, it would
never have got
past him. **99**

**Graham Gooch, English cricketer,
on Mike Gatting, who appeared
for England in 79 Test matches,
23 of them as captain between
1986 and 1988.**

> **Naseem Hamed is naturally fit. I've seen more fat on a butcher's apron.**

Reg Gutteridge, boxing commentator, on Naseem Hamed, English boxer, known as 'Prince Naseem', former World Featherweight and World Bantamweight champion.

Prince Naseem Hamed prepares to defend his featherweight title against Billy Hardy in Manchester. Hamed would win with a technical knockout and retain the title.
1997

" If some angel comes to me in my sleep and says, 'You are going to win Wimbledon, but you are not able to touch the racket ever again in your life,' I would say, 'OK, I will never play tennis again.' **"**

Goran Ivanisevic, Croatian tennis player, former World Number Two, winner of Wimbledon men's singles title in 2001.

Goran Ivanisevic shouts at his racquet in frustration during a match with Thomas Muster at the Ford Australian Open Championships, Melbourne.
22nd January, 1997

Eric Cantona, French footballer and actor, voted Manchester United's player of the century in 2001.

Manchester United's Eric Cantona, closely followed by David Beckham, celebrates the second goal against the Portuguese club Porto during their UEFA Champions League match at Old Trafford. United would win 4–0.
5th March, 1997

" When the seagulls follow the trawler, it is because they think sardines will be thrown into the sea. "

Jackie Stewart, head of his own team, Stewart Racing, during practice for the San Marino Grand Prix in Italy.
25th April, 1997

66 When I was young, motor racing was dangerous and sex was safe... now it is the other way round. **99**

Jackie Stewart, Scottish racing driver and team owner, three-times Formula 1 World Champion.

Old rivals Damon Hill (R) and Michael Schumacher confront each other at the Silverstone circuit in Northamptonshire before the British Grand Prix.
10th July, 1997

66 If I am pushed I will push back, that is the way I am. I am very British. We don't like to be pushed around. When the chips are down we might have to step into grey areas. 99

Damon Hill, English racing driver, former Formula 1 World Champion, president of British Racing Drivers' Club, son of two times Formula 1 World Champion Graham Hill.

66 I find this accusation so horrendous, so monstrous, that I have decided to confront it head-on by talking to the Press. I am frustrated and angry. I believe that I am absolutely 100 per cent innocent. I assure you: I have never taken drugs. 99

Martina Hingis, Swiss tennis player, former World Number One, winner of five Grand Slam women's singles titles and nine Grand Slam women's doubles titles, on testing positive for cocaine at Wimbledon in 2007. Despite her denial, she decided not to appeal the impending ban from playing.

Swiss player **Martina Hingis** serves during the US Open. She would win the final against a young Venus Williams and become the undisputed Women's Number One in 1997 by winning all but one Grand Slam tournament.
5th September, 1997

66 I'm five short (of the Arsenal goal scoring record), not that I'm counting. 99

Ian Wright, English footballer and television personality, who made 33 appearances for England, played 581 league games and scored 387 goals.

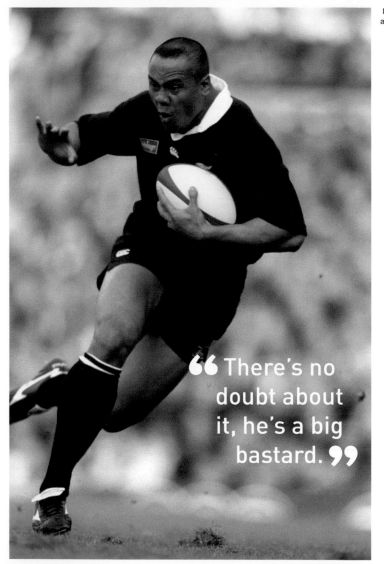

New Zealand's Jonah Lomu during a match against England at Old Trafford, Manchester. *22nd November, 1997*

❝ There's no doubt about it, he's a big bastard. ❞

Gavin Hastings, rugby player, on New Zealand player Jonah Lomu, who made 63 appearances for his national team and is regarded as one of the sport's most intimidating players.

" I've never wanted to leave. I'm here for the rest of my life, and hopefully after that as well. **"**

Alan Shearer, English footballer and television pundit, one of England's best ever strikers who made 63 appearances for the national team.

Newcastle United's Alan Shearer strikes a shot against the post during the FA Cup final against Arsenal at Wembley Stadium.
16th May, 1998

66 People go on about my foul on Simeone and the red card, but I'd obviously rather people talk about me scoring the penalty four years later. 99

David Beckham, English footballer, holder of the all-time appearance record (115) with the national team, captain of England between 2000 and 2006.

Former world champion sprinter Linford Christie leaves the High Court where he had won his libel claim against John McVicar, who had alleged that he had taken performance enhancing drugs to cheat his way to the top.
3rd July, 1998

James Christie, on the accusation that his son, English sprinter Linford Christie, had been taking performance enhancing drugs.

66 My son Linford does not use drugs. If they said he was taking roast chicken and baked potatoes then I would believe that. **99**

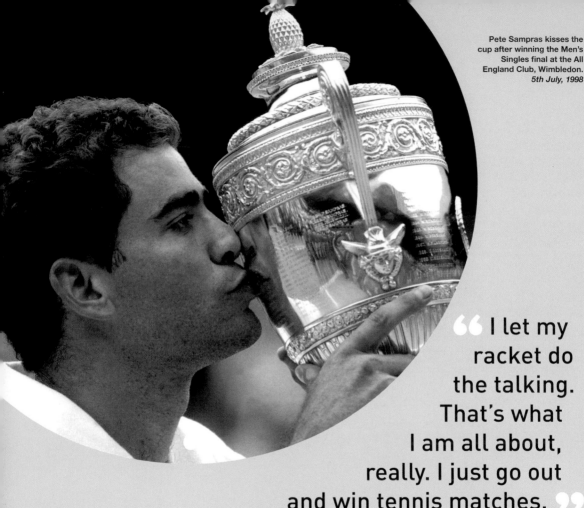

66 I let my
racket do
the talking.
That's what
I am all about,
really. I just go out
and win tennis matches. 99

**Pete Sampras, US tennis player, former
World Number One, winner of 14 Grand
Slam men's singles titles.**

> 66 I am not motivated by recognition, I just do things I like doing – racing, shagging, eating and drinking. 99

David Coulthard, Scottish racing driver and television commentator, winner of 13 Formula 1 Grands Prix.

Scot David Coulthard (R) shares a joke with McLaren team boss Ron Dennis during preparations for the Belgian Grand Prix at the Spa-Francorchamps circuit.
28th August, 1998

Veteran jockey Lester Piggott rides Desert Orchid past the stands during Wincanton Races.
25th October, 1998

66 People ask me why I ride with my bottom in the air. Well, I've got to put it somewhere. **99**

Lester Piggott, English jockey, known as 'The Long Fellow', the greatest flat jockey of all time with 4,493 career wins, including nine Derby victories.

Mark Williams looks despondent as Stephen Hendry wraps up the final of the Embassy World Snooker Championship, at The Crucible Theatre, Sheffield.
3rd May, 1999

66 It's like my living room, I put my pipe and slippers on and get my feet under the table. 99

Stephen Hendry, Scottish snooker player, former World Number One (for eight consecutive years), seven times World Champion.

Germany's Boris Becker clearly feels the strain during his match against Miles MacLagan at the All England Club, Wimbledon. He would go on to lose against Patrick Rafter in the fourth round.
22nd June, 1999

66 Tennis is a psychological sport; you have to keep a clear head. That is why I stopped playing. 99

Boris Becker, German tennis player, former World Number One and winner of six Grand Slam men's singles titles, youngest winner of the Men's Singles title at Wimbledon, Olympic gold medallist.

George Best during the FIFA World Player 1999 Awards Gala, in Brussels, Belgium. *24th January, 2000*

❝ It's a pleasure to be standing here. It's a pleasure to be standing up. ❞

George Best, Northern Irish footballer, on being voted 11th in the European Footballer of the Century election and 16th in the World Player of the Century election: Best's celebrity lifestyle had led to alcoholism that blighted his brilliant playing career.

American boxer Mike Tyson (L) throws a punch at Britain's Julius Francis, during their heavyweight fight at the MEN Arena, Manchester. Tyson would dispose of his challenger in four minutes, the referee stopping the bout in the second round.
29th January, 2000

66 My power is discombobulatingly devastating. I could feel his muscle tissues collapse under my force. It's ludicrous these mortals even attempt to enter my realm. 99

Mike Tyson, US heavyweight boxer, known as 'Iron Mike' and 'The Baddest Man on the Planet", first boxer to hold the WBA, WBC and IBF world heavyweight titles simultaneously, renowned for his intimidating and controversial behaviour both in and out of the ring.

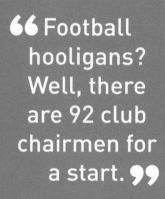

66 Football hooligans? Well, there are 92 club chairmen for a start. 99

Brian Clough, English footballer and team manager, remembered for being outspoken and often controversial, and considered by many to be the greatest English manager never to have managed the English team.

Seve Ballesteros blasts out of a bunker during the Eurobet Seve Ballesteros Trophy 2000 Tournament at Sunningdale, Berkshire. *14th April, 2000*

66 I look into their eyes, shake their hand, pat their back and wish them luck, but I am thinking, 'I am going to bury you.' **99**

Seve Ballesteros, Spanish golfer, former World Number One, three times winner of the Open Championship and twice winner of The Masters.

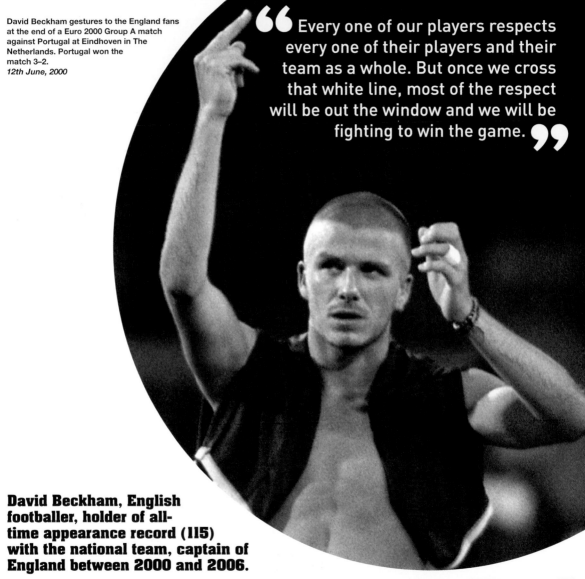

David Beckham gestures to the England fans at the end of a Euro 2000 Group A match against Portugal at Eindhoven in The Netherlands. Portugal won the match 3–2.
12th June, 2000

66 Every one of our players respects every one of their players and their team as a whole. But once we cross that white line, most of the respect will be out the window and we will be fighting to win the game. **99**

David Beckham, English footballer, holder of all-time appearance record (115) with the national team, captain of England between 2000 and 2006.

England goalkeeper David Seaman pounces on the ball during a Euro 2000 Group A match against Germany.
17th June, 2000

That Seaman is a handsome young man, but he spends too much time looking in his mirror, rather than at the ball. You can't keep goal with hair like that.

Brian Clough, football manager, on England goalkeeper David Seaman, who made 75 appearances for the national team.

Ethiopia's Haile Gebrselassie in action in the Men's 10,000m final at the Sydney Olympic Games in Australia.
September, 2000

"This is what I wanted. They tell me that London is the best field in history. I wanted to be part of that. Because everyone will be there, it will be a wonderful challenge for me. You can see the best runners, how they look, how they run. For me to beat the best is what counts."

Haile Gebrselassie, Ethiopian long-distance runner, 10,000m gold medallist at the 1996 and 2000 Olympic Games, winner of four 10,000m world championships, four times winner of the Berlin Marathon, three times winner of the Dubai Marathon.

Kenya's Paul Tergat waves to the crowd before the Men's 10,000m final during the Sydney Olympic Games in Australia. *September, 2000*

KENYA

Sydney 2000

2393

66 Ask yourself: 'Can I give more?' The answer is usually: 'Yes'. **99**

Paul Tergat, Kenyan long-distance runner, holder of Marathon world record from 2003 to 2007, 10,000m silver medallist at the 1996 and 2000 Olympic Games.

" **There is nothing going to stop me in the Sydney Olympics ... except me.** "

Marion Jones, US sprinter and long jumper, who subsequently admitted taking performance enhancing drugs and was stripped of three gold medals and two bronze medals won at Sydney in 2000.

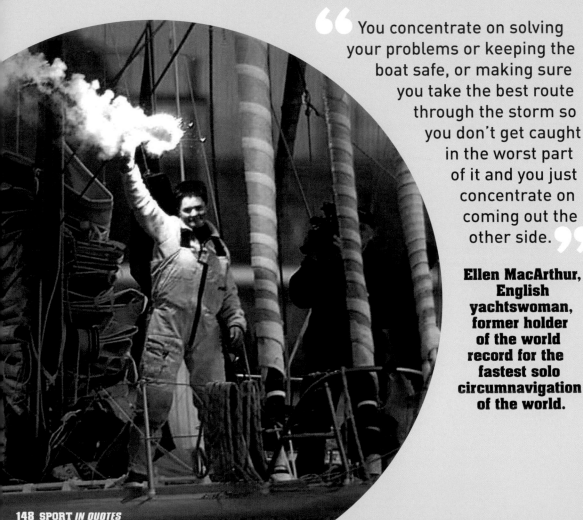

Ellen MacArthur arrives in Southampton after her record-breaking finish in the Vendée Globe race. The 24-year-old from Derbyshire became the youngest person and the fastest woman to circumnavigate the world single-handed.
15th February, 2001

66 You concentrate on solving your problems or keeping the boat safe, or making sure you take the best route through the storm so you don't get caught in the worst part of it and you just concentrate on coming out the other side. 99

Ellen MacArthur, English yachtswoman, former holder of the world record for the fastest solo circumnavigation of the world.

England's Ronnie O'Sullivan pots his way into the final of the World Snooker Championship during his semi-final match against Northern Ireland's Joe Swail, at the Crucible Theatre, Sheffield. *5th May, 2001*

66 Whoever called snooker 'chess with balls' was rude, but right. 99

Clive James, writer and broadcaster, on the sport of snooker.

South Africa's Gary Player putts on the 17th hole during a practice round for the Senior British Open Championship at Royal County Down, Northern Ireland.
25th July, 2001

❝ It's a marriage. If I had to choose between my wife and my putter, well, I'd miss her. ❞

Gary Player, South African golfer, winner of 165 tournaments on six continents over six decades, including three Masters, one US Open, three Open Championships and two PGA Championships.

David Beckham (L) with his BBC Sports Personality of the Year Award 2001 and Manchester United manager Sir Alex Ferguson with his Lifetime Achievement Award at BBC Television Centre, London. *9th December, 2001*

66 Alex Ferguson is the best manager I've ever had at this level. Well, he's the only manager I've actually had at this level. But he's the best manager I've ever had. 99

David Beckham, English footballer, on Manchester United manager Sir Alex Ferguson.

Former World Champion Niki Lauda, boss of the Jaguar Racing Formula 1 team, during qualifying for the British Grand Prix at Silverstone in Northamptonshire.
6th July, 2002

" You appreciate that it is very easy to die and you have to arrange your life to cope with that reality. "

Niki Lauda, Austrian racing driver and team manager, three times Formula 1 world champion.

Great Britain's long jumper Jonathan Edwards (37) announces his retirement from competition during a press conference in Paris, France.
22nd August, 2003

66 I was always dismissive of sports psychology when I was competing, but I now realize that my belief in God was sports psychology in all but name. **99**

Jonathan Edwards, English triple jumper, Olympic gold medallist; former Commonwealth, European and World champion; world record holder. Edwards was reported as having rejected Christianity in 2007.

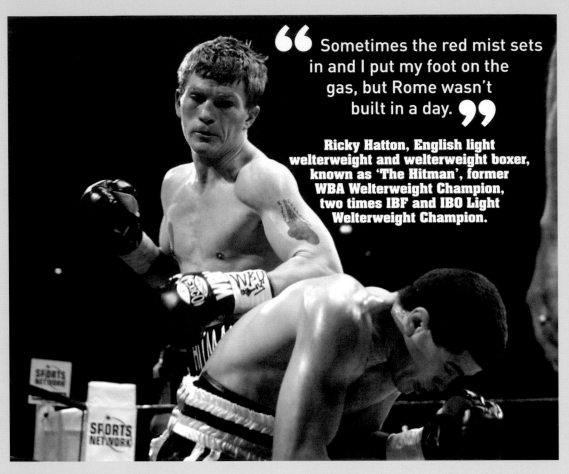

66 Sometimes the red mist sets in and I put my foot on the gas, but Rome wasn't built in a day. 99

Ricky Hatton, English light welterweight and welterweight boxer, known as 'The Hitman', former WBA Welterweight Champion, two times IBF and IBO Light Welterweight Champion.

Ricky Hatton (L) lands a left to Argentina's Aldo Rios during a WBU Light Welterweight world title bout at the MEN Arena in Manchester. *27th September, 2003*

Before a match I like to relax with 25 bottles of Holsten Pils and six steak 'n' kidney pies.

Andy Fordham, English darts player, known as 'The Viking', winner of 2004 BDO World Darts Championship, on his MySpace page, 2007. Subsequent serious health concerns, which saw him put on a liver transplant list, led to Fordham losing 238lb.

Andy Fordham during his semi-final game against Raymond Van Barneveld in the World Professional Darts Championships at Lakeside Country Club, Frimley Green, Surrey. Fordham would go on to win the tournament by beating Mervyn King in the final.
10th January, 2004

66 When I do that, it means I'm not going to miss the ball. **99**

Maria Sharapova, Russian tennis player, former World Number One, winner of three Grand Slam women's singles titles, on screaming.

Maria Sharapova from Russia roars after breaking American Serena Williams' serve in the second set of the final of the Women's Singles tournament at the All England Club, Wimbledon. *3rd July, 2004*

66 Well, if you take Roddick's serve, Agassi's return, my volley and Hewitt's speed, you've probably got a chance. 99

Tim Henman, English tennis player, when asked if anyone could challenge Swiss player Roger Federer at the US Open in 2004.

Roger Federer from Switzerland in action before defeating the USA's Andy Roddick in the final of the Men's Singles tournament at the All England Club, Wimbledon.
4th July, 2004

“ They have a few drinks and probably the prawn sandwiches, and they don't realize what's going on out on the pitch. I don't think some of the people who come to Old Trafford can spell football, never mind understand it. **”**

Roy Keane, Irish footballer and team manager, noted for his aggressive and highly competitive style of playing, captain of Manchester United for eight years.

Manchester United's captain, Roy Keane, playing at centre-half looks for answers after Chelsea's opening goal during an FA Barclays Premiership match at Stamford Bridge, London.
15th August, 2004

66 For myself, losing is not coming second. It's getting out of the water knowing you could have done better. For myself, I have won every race I've been in. **99**

Ian Thorpe, Australian freestyle swimmer, known as the 'Thorpedo', winner of three gold medals (400m Freestyle, 4 x 100m Freestyle Relay and 4 x 200m Freestyle Relay) at the 2000 Sydney Olympic Games and two gold medals (200m and 400m Freestyle) at the 2004 Athens Olympic Games, winner of 11 World Championship gold medals.

Australian swimmer Ian Thorpe celebrates after winning a gold medal in the Men's 200m Freestyle event at the Olympic Aquatic Centre during the Athens Olympic Games, Greece.
16th August, 2004

66 It was so hot out there, if I had been able to run naked I would have. Unfortunately I could not because I knew my ten-year-old daughter would be watching! **99**

Catherine Ndereba, Kenyan long-distance runner, Marathon silver medallist at the 2004 Athens and 2008 Beijing Olympic Games, four times winner of the Boston Marathon, USA.

Kenya's Catherine Ndereba comes home to win silver in the Marathon during the Athens Olympic Games in Greece.
22nd August, 2004

> **Sometimes, when I walk out on to the track I think, 'What am I doing here? Why do I put myself through this?' But that's when you really get into your focus... you focus on the race you are going to run.**

Kelly Holmes, English middle-distance runner, 800m and 1500m gold medallist at the 2004 Athens Olympic Games.

Great Britain's Kelly Holmes (C) crosses the finishing line to win gold in the Women's 800m final during the Athens Olympic Games in Greece. Also pictured are Morocco's Hasna Benhassi (L), who came second, and Maria de Lurdes Mutola from Mozambique.
23rd August, 2004

66 I've broken my nose a couple of times, my thumb, my forearm, my shoulders, my ankle... I could go on and on! 99

Gareth Thomas, Welsh rugby player, who has made 100 rugby union and four rugby league appearances for Wales, second highest try scorer for Wales.

Wales' Gareth Thomas receives treatment for an injury to his thumb during a Six Nations match against France at the Stade de France, Paris. *26th February, 2005*

> **Every time I go out and race it's a goal to go out and run faster than I've done before.**

Paula Radcliffe, English long-distance runner, Marathon world record holder, Marathon gold medallist at the 2005 Helsinki Olympic Games.

Great Britain's Paula Radcliffe crosses the finishing line to win the Women's Marathon during the IAAF World Athletics Championships at the Olympic Stadium in Helsinki, Finland.
14th August, 2005

66 Forwards are the gnarled and scarred creatures who have a propensity for running into and bleeding all over each other. 99

Peter Fitzsimmons, Australian rugby player, writer and broadcaster.

Leeds Tykes' forwards Jordan Crane (L), Gavin Kerr and Scott Morgan (R) line up to tackle Cardiff Blues' Craig Quinnell (C) during the Heineken Cup match at Cardiff Arms Park, Cardiff.
22nd October, 2005

❝ One accusation
you can't throw
at me is that I've
always done my best. ❞

**Alan Shearer, English footballer and
television pundit, one of England's
best ever strikers who made 63
appearances for the national team.**

Belgium's Kim Clijsters in action against Russia's Vera Zvonareva during the first round of the Lawn Tennis Championships at the All England Club, Wimbledon.
27th June, 2006

66 You know, my ankles, my wrists, everything is just sore and making a lot of noise... I'm 22, but my body is not 22 any more. 99

Kim Clijsters, Belgian tennis player, former World Number One, winner of four Grand Slam women's singles titles and runner-up in four more.

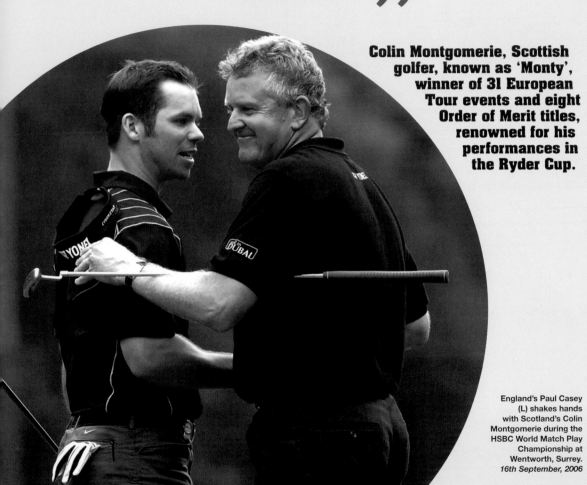

> ❝ To be truthful, I think golfers are overpaid. It's unreal, and I have trouble dealing with the guilt sometimes. ❞

Colin Montgomerie, Scottish golfer, known as 'Monty', winner of 31 European Tour events and eight Order of Merit titles, renowned for his performances in the Ryder Cup.

England's Paul Casey (L) shakes hands with Scotland's Colin Montgomerie during the HSBC World Match Play Championship at Wentworth, Surrey. *16th September, 2006*

❝... I hope to maintain my credibility after I stop playing. Because, yes of course, now I play and I score goals, and children all over are mad about me. Not just poor children – all children. We can make them really happy by the way we play, though I have to say that it's the poor ones that I think of most, the ones who can't come and watch the games at the stadium. We mean so much to them. That's why I'm so committed to this work. Later, after you've stopped playing, it's harder to have the same impact. But I will give it a go. I want to continue doing this kind of work forever. **❞**

Christiano Ronaldo, Portuguese footballer, captain of Portugal, the most expensive player in history after moving from Manchester United to Real Madrid in an £80m transfer deal.

McLaren driver Lewis Hamilton in the pits at Silverstone, Northamptonshire, during the run-up to the British Grand Prix.
7th July, 2007

" The year I get here, he bales out – I don't know if I had something to do with that! "

Lewis Hamilton, racing driver, on seven-times World Champion Michael Schumacher, who had just retired from racing.

Former Ferrari F1 Champion Michael Schumacher, acting as an advisor to the team, is seen during a practice session for the European Grand Prix at the Nürburgring, Nürburg, Germany.
20th July, 2007

66 Those who have come into Formula One without experiencing cars devoid of electronic aids will find it tough. To control 800 horsepower relying just on arm muscles and foot sensitivity can turn out to be a dangerous exercise. 99

Michael Schumacher, German racing driver, seven times Formula 1 World Champion, only driver in Formula 1 history to have finished in the top three in every race of a season.

" I like to think I play rugby as it should be played – there are no yellow or red cards in my collection – but I cannot say I'm an angel. **"**

Jonny Wilkinson, English rugby player who has made 82 appearances for England, and six for the British and Irish Lions, one of the world's best rugby players.

England's Jonny Wilkinson carries the ball away from a tackle during a Pool A match against Samoa at the Stade de la Beaujoire, Nantes, France, during the IRB Rugby World Cup.
22nd September, 2007

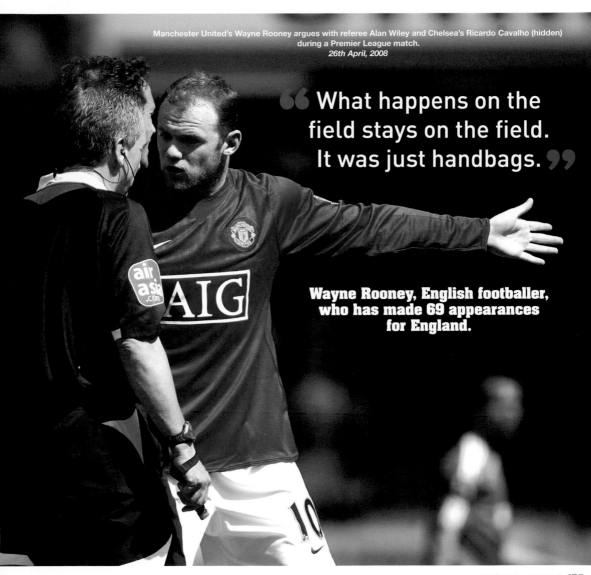

Manchester United's Wayne Rooney argues with referee Alan Wiley and Chelsea's Ricardo Cavalho (hidden) during a Premier League match.
26th April, 2008

" What happens on the field stays on the field. It was just handbags. "

Wayne Rooney, English footballer, who has made 69 appearances for England.

It's like a toaster, the ref's shirt pocket. Every time there's a tackle, up pops a yellow card.

**Kevin Keegan,
English footballer
and team manager
who made 63
appearances for
England,**

Newcastle United manager Kevin Keegan (L) confronts Chelsea's manager, Avram Grant (C), on the touchline during a Barclays Premier League match at St James' Park, Newcastle.
5th May, 2008

" It will be an honour to represent my country and get all the kit, stay in the Olympic village, and, when I'm old enough, get a tattoo with the Olympic rings. **"**

Tom Daley, English diver, 10m Synchro and 10m Individual diving gold medallist at the 2010 Commonwealth Games, Britain's youngest competitor at the 2008 Beijing Olympic Games at the age of 14.

" It's nice to be recognized for actually achieving something in life as opposed to spending seven weeks on TV in the *Big Brother* house with a load of other muppets. "

Bradley Wiggins, English cyclist, 4km Individual Pursuit gold medallist at the 2004 Athens Olympic Games, 4km Individual Pursuit and Team Pursuit gold medallist at the 2008 Beijing Olympic Games; took fourth place in the 2009 Tour de France.

Great Britain's Bradley Wiggins during the Men's Individual Pursuit final at the Loashan Velodrome during the Beijing Olympics, China. *16th August, 2008*

Usain Bolt of Jamaica is subjected to the cameraman's attention after winning the gold medal in the Men's 200m final at the National Stadium during the Beijing Olympic Games, China.
20th August, 2008

"I just blew my mind, and blew the world's mind."

Usain Bolt, Jamaican sprinter, 100m, 200m and 4 x 100m Relay gold medallist at the 2008 Beijing Olympic Games, 100m, 200m and 4 x 100m Relay World Champion 2009.

66 I remember the first time I walked into the Lancashire dressing-room, when I was 16, all these guys – Atherton, Fairbrother, Akram – you just drop your shopping, you don't know where to put yourself. With Botham, I could barely pick my shopping up. 99

Andrew Flintoff, English cricketer, on the first time he met Ian Botham, former England Test team captain who scored 14 centuries and took 383 wickets in Test cricket.

Olympic gold medallist Chris Hoy with the Knighthood he received from the Prince of Wales during an investiture at Buckingham Palace, London.
11th June, 2009

Chris Hoy, Scottish cyclist, winner of three gold medals at the 2008 Beijing Olympics, the most successful Olympic male cyclist of all time.

❝It's bizarre, it almost seems like it's not real. To become a knight from riding your bike, it's mad.❞

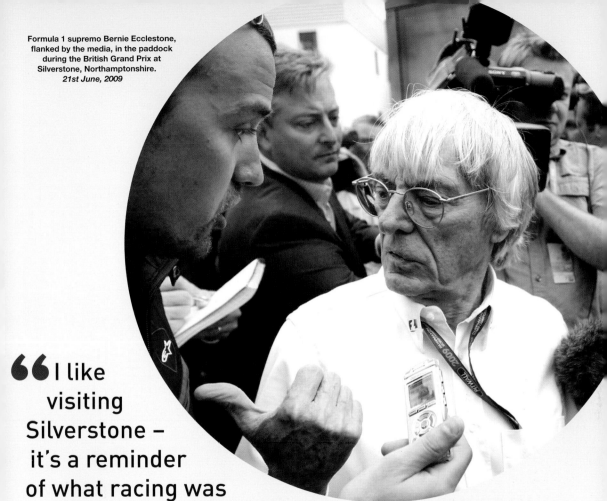

Formula 1 supremo Bernie Ecclestone, flanked by the media, in the paddock during the British Grand Prix at Silverstone, Northamptonshire. *21st June, 2009*

"I like visiting Silverstone – it's a reminder of what racing was like in the 1950s."

Bernie Ecclestone, president and CEO of Formula One Management and Formula One Administration.

Stirling Moss at the wheel of a restored Mercedes W196 Grand Prix car, dating from the mid-1950s, during the Goodwood Festival of Speed at Chichester, West Sussex.
5th July, 2009

" If God had meant for us to walk, why did he give us feet that fit car pedals? **"**

Stirling Moss, English racing driver, the greatest driver never to have won the World Championship.

USA's Tom Watson in action during practice day three for the Open Championship at Turnberry Golf Club, Scotland.
14th July, 2009

66 My golf swing is like ironing a shirt. You get one side smoothed out, turn it over and there is a big wrinkle on the other side. You iron that side, turn it over and there's another wrinkle. 99

Tom Watson, US golfer, former World Number One, winner of two Masters Tournaments, one US Open and five Open Championships.

England's David Beckham (C) in action with Belarus' Alexander Yurevich (L) during a Group 6 qualifying round for the FIFA World Cup at Wembley Stadium.
14th October, 2009

66 He cannot kick with his left foot, he cannot head a ball, he cannot tackle and he doesn't score many goals. Apart from that he's all right. **99**

George Best, Irish footballer, on David Beckham, holder of all-time appearance record (115) for England, captain of the national team between 2000 and 2006.

> **The sport would not survive today if drivers were being killed at the rate they were in the 1960s and '70s. It would have been taken off the air. It is beamed into people's living rooms on Sunday afternoons, with children watching.**

Damon Hill, English racing driver, former Formula 1 World Champion, president of British Racing Drivers' Club, son of two times Formula 1 World Champion Graham Hill.

Damon Hill (L) and Silverstone managing director Richard Phillips during a press conference at the Grosvenor House Hotel, London, to announce a new deal between the Northamptonshire circuit and Formula 1 supremo Bernie Ecclestone to save the British Grand Prix.
7th December, 2009

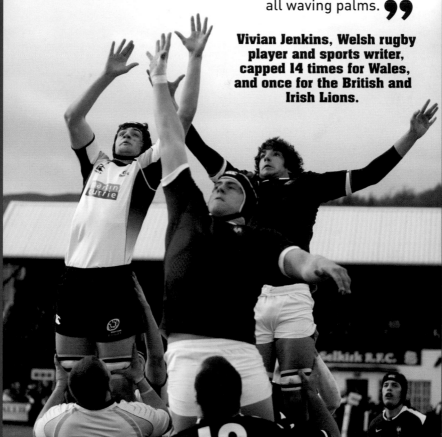

Scotland Under 18s'
Andrew Redmayne (L)
jumps in the lineout
during a match against
France U18 at Philiphaugh,
Selkirk, Scotland.
14th March, 2010

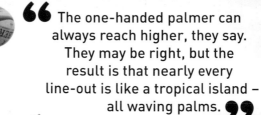

" The one-handed palmer can
always reach higher, they say.
They may be right, but the
result is that nearly every
line-out is like a tropical island –
all waving palms. "

**Vivian Jenkins, Welsh rugby
player and sports writer,
capped 14 times for Wales,
and once for the British and
Irish Lions.**

66 In the rainy season, sometimes to get to the first lesson we had to run really quick, because we had to cross the river to school and we'd have to go up and down the bank to find a place to cross because there is no bridge. 99

Haile Gebrselassie, Ethiopian long-distance runner, 10,000m gold medallist at the 1996 and 2000 Olympic Games, winner of four 10,000m world championships, four times winner of the Berlin Marathon, three times winner of the Dubai Marathon.

Ethiopia's Haile Gebrselassie celebrates crossing the line to win the elite men's race during the BUPA Great Manchester Run in Manchester. 16th May, 2010

> " Through my illness, I learned rejection. I was written off. That was the moment I thought, 'Okay, game on. No prisoners. Everybody's going down.' "

Lance Armstrong, US cyclist, seven times winner of the Tour de France.

Lance Armstrong of the USA finishes the Tour de France Preliminary Stage, Time Trial in Rotterdam, Netherlands. *3rd July, 2010*

66 As a kid, I might have been psycho, I guess, but I used to throw golf balls in the trees and try and somehow make par from them. I thought that was fun. 99

Tiger Woods, US golfer, formerly World Number One and the highest paid athlete in the world, winner of 14 major golf championships, 71 PGA Tour events and 16 World Golf Championships.

USA's Tiger Woods during his final practice round for the 38th Ryder Cup against Europe at the Celtic Manor Resort, Gwent, Wales.
30th September, 2010

The Publishers gratefully acknowledge Press Association Images, from whose extensive archives the photographs in this book have been selected. Personal copies of the photographs in this book, and many others, may be ordered online at www.prints.paphotos.com

AMMONITE PRESS

AE Publications Ltd, 166 High Street, Lewes, East Sussex, BN7 1XU, United Kingdom
Tel: +44 (0)1273 488006   Fax: +44 (0)1273 472418
www.ammonitepress.com